MW00851745

Published by Pleasant Company Publications

© Copyright 1995 by Pleasant Company

All rights reserved. No part of this book except the blackline masters may be used or reproduced in any manner
whatsoever without written permission except in the case of brief quotations embodied in critical articles and reviews.
For information, address: Book Editor, Pleasant Company Publications, 8400 Fairway Place, P.O. Box 620998, Middleton, WI 53562.

First Edition.
Printed in the United States of America.
95 96 97 98 99 WCR 10 9 8 7 6 5 4 3 2 1

The American Girls Collection® and Molly McIntire® are registered trademarks of Pleasant Company.

WORLD WAR TWO
★ OVERVIEW ★

ABOUT THE MOLLY BOOKS

Molly McIntire is a lively nine-year-old whose family is learning to live with war, just like every family in the United States in 1944. Home-front World War Two is the setting for all six books of historical fiction about Molly.

Cooperation stands out as one theme in the Molly books. Molly and her schoolmates work together to benefit soldiers, and Molly and her family make daily sacrifices in their lives while Dad is away at war. They're just like Americans everywhere on the home front, who joined volunteer groups and worked in factories to support the war. Similarly, as a nation, the United States pooled its resources with those of its allies. All these efforts of cooperation served one common cause: winning the war.

Change and *self-reliance* are other important themes in the Molly books. Molly must learn to be resourceful and responsible for herself. In this way, her stories parallel that of the United States as it, too, took on the larger responsibilities of a world power because of the war. Both Molly and her country must deal with changes and make peace with a world that will never be the same.

Apr.-June 1940 Germany takes over Denmark, Norway, Belgium, the Netherlands, and France.

Nov. 1940 President Franklin Roosevelt elected to third term.

Dec. 7, 1941 Japan bombs Pearl Harbor. The U.S. enters the war.

1939	1940	1941	194:

Sept. 1939 World War Two begins when Germany invades Poland.

Sept. 1940 The Blitz begins (the German bombing of London).

Apr.-June 1941 Germany invades Greece, Yugoslavia, and the Soviet Union.

Jan. 194 Rationing begins in the U.S.

THE HISTORICAL CONTEXT

The First World War (1914-18) was supposed to be "the war to end all wars." But afterward, dictators took over in Italy, the Soviet Union, Spain, Germany, and Japan. During the 1930s, they harnessed the national and racial prejudices of their citizens to build powerful armies and launch wars. On September 1, 1939, German dictator Adolf Hitler ordered his army to invade Poland. Within weeks, war engulfed most nations of the world.

Most Americans wanted to stay out of World War Two, though they clearly favored the Allies—led by England, France, and the Soviet Union—over the Axis Powers led by Germany, Japan, and Italy. Instead of sending troops, President Roosevelt donated billions of dollars' worth of arms and supplies to the Allies.

In 1941, the Japanese attacked Pearl Harbor, a U.S. naval base in Hawaii, killing more than 2,400 Americans. The attack finally thrust the United States into the war. The day after the attack, Congress voted to declare war on Japan. Before the week was over, Germany and Italy, fulfilling their treaties with Japan, declared war on the United States. The country now faced two wars—one against fascism in Europe and the other against Japanese imperialism in Asia. During the next four years, more than sixteen million Americans served in the military. By war's end, more than 400,000 had given their lives to the cause.

ABOUT THE AUTHOR
Valerie Tripp did some of the research for the Molly books by talking to her parents. Her father fought in the army during World War Two. Her mother lived on the home front and told her all about war bonds and rationing. Students interested in learning more about Ms. Tripp will enjoy blackline master 1 (page 7 of this book).

MOLLY'S LIFE

1934 April 22
Molly is born.

1943 October-November
Meet Molly takes place.

1943 November
Molly Learns a Lesson

1943 December
Molly's Surprise

1944 April
Happy Birthday, Molly!

1944 April 22
Molly turns 10.

1944 June-July
Molly Saves the Day

1945 March
Changes for Molly

Nov. 1942
Allies land in Africa to gain bases for invading Europe.

Sept. 1943
Allies begin invasion of southern Europe.

July 1944
Allies first see Nazi death camps.

Nov. 1944
Roosevelt elected to fourth term.

May 7, 1945
Germany surrenders.

Aug. 6 & 9, 1945 U.S. drops atomic bombs on two Japanese cities, Hiroshima and Nagasaki.

1943   **1944**   **1945**

...e 1942
defeats
...nese
at Battle
...idway.
... never
...ers.

Feb. 1943
Soviets defeat the German army in the battle of Stalingrad. The tide of the war turns against Germany.

June 6, 1944
D-Day. Allies land in Normandy, France, to begin invasion of northern Europe.

June-July 1944
U.S. defeats Japan at Mariana Islands and then uses the islands as bases for flying bombing missions to Japan.

April 12, 1945
Roosevelt dies. Harry Truman becomes president.

Sept. 2, 1945
Japan surrenders.

The Office of Civil Defense insignia

MOLLY'S HOMETOWN

After the bombing of Pearl Harbor, American communities rallied for the war effort, just as Molly's fictional town, Jefferson, Illinois, does. Towns that had suffered record unemployment during the Depression of the 1930s suddenly had jobs for everyone. Some towns in the Midwest were transformed by the construction of army bases, factories, airfields, and temporary barracks thrown together for workers and servicemen. Stars began to appear in the windows of homes—a blue star for each family member fighting in the war, a gold star for each member killed. Songs like "Good-bye, Mama, I'm off to Yokohama" filled the radio waves. Air-raid sirens announced drills and blackouts so that everyone could practice for enemy attacks.

Citizens at home made do with less as factories began to produce war materials rather than consumer goods. Detroit stopped making cars during the war to make tanks, trucks, aircraft, and ships instead. Things made from some materials, like rubber, became almost impossible to find. Motorists drove their cars sparingly and slowly to save tires. Many products, from sugar to shoes, were rationed. Most Americans respected rationing rules, though black markets flourished for those willing to pay a premium for scarce goods.

Americans flocked to the movies during the war. One of the landmarks of Molly's town, as in many American cities at the time, was the ornate downtown movie "palace." Newsreels before the feature showed real, moving pictures of the war, which touched nearly every family but was fought so far away. Moviegoers hungered for dramas about the war. Hollywood responded by cranking out over 500 war films between 1942 and 1945. These and other movies encouraged the values so esteemed by the nation at war—values like patriotism, thrift, grit, and community spirit.

ABOUT HISTORICAL FICTION

The stories about Molly were made up by Valerie Tripp— but within a rigorously researched world of historical fact. Indeed, it's the combination of historical accuracy and a well-told tale that makes historical fiction such a compelling way for children to learn about the past.

To do the research for the Molly books, Ms. Tripp studied the books, movies, music, magazines, and catalogues of the period. Most of all, she talked to people who lived through the war, both on the home front and the battle-front. Ms. Tripp says that two impressions stand out from all these conversations: that the war affected everyone, and that citizens pulled together and sacrificed for the greater good. The many people she talked to remember with fondness and even longing the feeling of unity that arose from having a common purpose.

USING THE PICTURE MAP

The picture map enables children to make a multitude of comparisons between life in Molly's time and life today. They can compare modes of transportation then and now, types of clothing, and architectural styles. You can also use the map before students read the books (except *Molly Saves the Day*) to point out places where events in the stories take place. Display it while students work on projects described on TG pages 46-59. Use it as part of a unit on World War Two. Here are some important ideas about towns like Molly's that the map makes evident:

Wartime changes The aircraft factory on the outskirts of Jefferson and the temporary housing around it show the effects of the war. So do the Victory gardens that replaced lawns. Because of shortages of fuel and tires, even horse-drawn vehicles reappeared. Notice the horse-drawn car near the railroad station. Patriotism displays itself, too, in flags and bunting and on billboards and other signs.

The importance of downtown In Molly's time, down-town was the center of community life—of shopping, office work, moviegoing, and transportation. It wasn't until the 1950s and 1960s that the great boom in suburban housing and automobile use began pulling commercial activity to the edges of cities, and downtowns began deteriorating.

The "gridiron pattern" In the mid-1900s, many Mid-western towns had—and many still have—regular street plans like Jefferson's. In parts of the nation that were settled earlier than the Midwest, streets often follow streams or other natural features, colonial or Indian footpaths, and even ancient fortifications (as Wall Street in New York City does). But the Northwest Ordinance of 1785 required the territories of Minnesota, Wisconsin,

READING THE BOOKS
IN SEQUENCE
*Students don't need to read all six books about Molly or to read the books in sequence. Each book makes sense on its own. But students will have a deeper understanding of Molly's life and times if they **do** read the books in order, since certain events in earlier books cause or affect events in later books.*

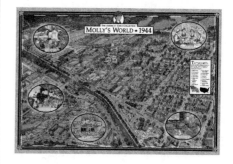

PAGE REFERENCES
Most page numbers in this guide refer to pages in the Molly books. References to teacher's guide pages are marked "TG"— for example, "on TG pages 46-59."

Illinois, Indiana, Michigan, and Ohio to be surveyed and divided in a regular way. So townships in the territories were laid out in six-mile squares, following lines of latitude and longitude. Subsequent surveying and development usually followed these established lines.

Blackline masters 2-3 on TG pages 8-9 acquaint students with the map so they can use it independently.

INTRODUCING VOCABULARY

A list of vocabulary words has been provided for each book. (See TG pages 10, 16, 22, 28, 34, and 40.) Words were chosen for the following reasons:

- They are important to the meaning of the story.
- They are likely to be unfamiliar to students.
- The meaning of the words isn't obvious from context.
- Students are likely to encounter the words elsewhere.

You could preview vocabulary words with students before they read or discuss the words after reading—or do both. Students could also add words to the list as they read. The activities below offer ways to engage students in vocabulary study.

Play Vocabulary Concentration. Make a set of cards with a vocabulary word on each card. On another set of cards, write definitions of the words. Mix the cards together and lay them in rows, face down. Have students turn over cards, two at a time, to try to match a word and its definition. Students who make matches can continue their turn.

Create analogies. Have students create analogies that illustrate the meaning of vocabulary words (*superior : inferior :: high : low*). After creating the analogies, students could omit the vocabulary words and ask other students to finish the incomplete analogies.

Make a wall of word webs. Have students put a vocabulary word in the center of a space on a chalkboard or bulletin board. Have them create a word web around it by writing synonyms, antonyms, and related words. For example, *attractive* and *fashionable* could be synonyms linked to the vocabulary word *glamorous*.

Create vocabulary quotes. Assign each vocabulary word to a student. Have students create quotes for the day that use the words. Each quote should capture the meaning of the word while also expressing a truism, observation, or bit of philosophy.

From the Author: *Valerie Tripp*

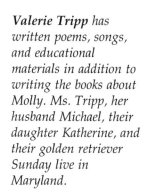

Me at age eight.

"I liked school, especially reading. Like Molly, I loved the teachers and always wanted to be the star of the school play, to write the best story, and to win the spelling bee. Also, just like Molly, I was terrible at multiplication!"

What are you best at in school? What do you wish you were better at?

_____

_____

Valerie Tripp has written poems, songs, and educational materials in addition to writing the books about Molly. Ms. Tripp, her husband Michael, their daughter Katherine, and their golden retriever Sunday live in Maryland.

"I used to feel awkward because I was always the tallest one in my class. I was afraid I daydreamed too much. And my hair never looked exactly the way I wanted it to, so I fussed with it—just as Molly fusses with her hair in *Changes for Molly*.

"Pay close attention to your hopes and daydreams. Everything that is happening to you right now and everything you are thinking about is important. You must be especially observant and thoughtful if you would like to be a writer, because your memories and your imagination will be your best source of ideas."

Which of your hopes or daydreams might make a good story?

_____

_____

Valerie Tripp

Name _____

Using the Map, "Molly's World, 1944"

The map gives you lots of information about what it was like to live in a town like Jefferson, Illinois, during World War Two. The more you look at the map, the more you'll see! The questions and activities below will help you use the map.

1. Look at the map to get familiar with it. Then write one or two questions you have about Molly's world.

_____

_____

_____

2. Read the paragraph in the box on the right side of the map. Then read the *legend*—the list of numbers and labels below the paragraph. The legend tells you that Willow Street School is number 6. Find number 6 on the map. Write down the names of the three streets that surround the school.

_____

_____

3. Notice the map of the United States below the legend. The dot stands for Jefferson, Illinois. Draw a dot on this map to show where you live.

4. Look at the compass rose at the bottom of the map. It shows directions. In what direction would Molly walk to get from Willow Street School to the railroad station?

_____

Continued on blackline master 3.

Name _____

Using the Map *Continued*

5. Notice the five "close-ups" on the map—the pictures that show you details about certain places. Look at the close-up of Molly's classroom. List at least three ways her classroom is like yours and three ways it is different.

Ways Molly's Classroom Is Like Mine	**Ways Molly's Classroom Is Different from Mine**
_____	_____
_____	_____
_____	_____

6. If you look closely at the map, you'll find one example of an old form of transportation. (If you need help finding it, use the clue at the bottom of this page.) What is this old form of transportation? Why do you think it was sometimes used during World War Two?

_____

_____

7. The map shows pictures of many things related to World War Two. List four things you see on the map that relate to the war.

_____

_____

8. Look again at the questions you wrote on blackline master 2. Can you use the map to answer your questions? If not, how can you figure out the answers? If necessary, ask your teacher or librarian for help, and then answer them.

_____

_____

Clue: Look just below and to the right of the railroad station.

MEET ★ MOLLY ★

AN AMERICAN GIRL

USING THE PICTURE MAP

Before students start to read **Meet Molly,** *use the picture map to orient them to Molly's world. Point out her house and neighborhood and the Red Cross, where Molly's mother works as a volunteer.*

VOCABULARY WORDS

You could introduce the words before students read the book or after they finish. See TG page 6 for activities. The words are shown with the page where they first appear.

superior (4): snobby
tended (10): cared for
unpatriotic (11): disloyal to country
pact (17): agreement
glamorous (29): attractive
indignantly (40): angrily

THE ALOHA STATE

In 1944, Hawaii was not yet a state, though it had been a U.S. territory since 1900. Hawaii played an important role for the United States in World War Two because of the attack on Pearl Harbor and Hawaii's strategic value in the Pacific.

PLOT SUMMARY

Chapter 1 Nine-year-old Molly McIntire is still sitting at the kitchen table long after her older sister Jill and brothers Ricky and Brad have finished their dinners—including turnips from the Victory garden. Until Molly eats her turnips, Mrs. Gilford, the housekeeper, won't let her leave the table. Molly thinks about how things have changed since Dad went to England seven months ago to treat wounded soldiers. Later, when Mom comes home from work at the Red Cross, she reminds Molly that even though the war has changed some things, other things—like Mom and "olly Molly"—are still the same.

Chapter 2 Molly and her two best friends are planning their Halloween costumes. It's a challenge, because wartime shortages have made so many materials unobtainable. After Ricky teases them, they tease him about Jill's friend Dolores—the girl Ricky has a crush on. Ricky vows to get revenge on the three girls, but Molly soon forgets all about the threat as she practices the hula for her debut as a Hawaiian dancer on Halloween.

Chapter 3 Mom helps Molly and her friends make grass skirts out of paper, and they adorn themselves with paper flowers and go trick-or-treating. Though rationing means that the girls don't get many sweets, they still come home with lots of goodies. Just as they reach the door, Ricky exacts his revenge by drenching them with water. The grass skirts and Halloween treats are ruined. Molly promises Ricky he will be sorry, and she and her friends go inside to plan their revenge.

Chapter 4 Mom finds out about Ricky's attack with the hose and punishes him, but Molly and her friends feel he gets off too easily. They go ahead with their own plan for revenge. The next day, while Ricky watches in horror, the three girls throw his underwear out the window—right onto the heads of Jill and Dolores. After seeing the mess,

Mom orders the tricks to stop and metes out punishments. She reminds the children that though their tricks may not seem serious, it's meanness and revenge that starts wars. As they clean up, Molly and Ricky agree to be friends, and peace reigns on the home front once more.

THEMES IN THE STORY

Cooperation Molly struggles to cooperate in this story and the others. She must bring her own desires in line with realistic expectations and other people's desires. She must be an ally, just as the nation had to be. In this story, teasing from Ricky (pages 11-12, 22-23) escalates into a war until Mom intervenes. She tells Molly and Ricky that "meanness, anger, and revenge" start wars (page 50). The childen agree to stop fighting and decide that it's better to be friends than enemies (pages 51-52).

Continuity and change Before the war, Molly felt safe at home and secure in her routines. Mom wasn't at the Red Cross every day, and Molly didn't have to eat turnips. Since Dad left for the war, there are no more family dinners (pages 5-6) or "I'm home" hugs (page 8). The loss of security Molly feels was felt worldwide. Even so, some things remain the same for Molly, like Ricky's teasing and the fun of Halloween. Just as the nation struggles to cope with changes brought by war while maintaining old traditions and daily life, Molly and her family work to balance continuity and change.

"LOOKING BACK" SUMMARY

"Looking Back" describes life in America in Molly's day.

• In Molly's time, many Americans listened to the radio for news and entertainment.

• The United States entered World War Two after the Japanese attacked Pearl Harbor.

• Almost every family in the United States had a friend or relative who went to war.

• American factories "went to war" by making military supplies rather than products like cars and toys.

• Many women went to work in the factories to do the jobs left by men fighting in the war.

• People who stayed at home did what they could to help the war effort.

SPOT ART IN THE
MOLLY BOOKS

Spot illustrations like the ones on pages 4-5 and 22-23 hark back to the style of animation that was becoming popular in Molly's time. Objects are shown to have feelings—the turnips seem to be disgusted, for example. The objects and feelings reinforce the meaning of the passages they illustrate.

WARTIME PRESSURES
ON FAMILIES

In 1943, when the need for recruits increased, married men were drafted into the armed services. Between 1940 and 1945, the number of families headed by a married woman with an absent husband increased from 770,000 to almost three million. Many mothers had to leave children alone when they went to work. Some children sat in cars in factory parking lots, others spent the days in movie theaters, and some were locked into their homes.

Name _____

Before Reading *Meet Molly*

Look through *Meet Molly*. By looking at the cover, the portraits of Molly's family and friends, the story and pictures, and the pages that come before and after the story, you can learn a lot about the book. Then answer the questions below.

1. The story takes place in 1944, during World War Two. Jot down at least three things you know or would like to know about that time in American history.

_____

_____

_____

2. Look at the pictures of Molly on the cover and inside the book. Based on these pictures, what kind of person do you think Molly is?

_____

_____

3. Here's a word that's important in the story: *revenge*. Give an example to show what *revenge* means.

_____

_____

4. What questions do you have about the characters, setting, or plot of *Meet Molly*? Write at least two questions that you expect the story to answer.

_____

_____

_____

Name _____

As You Read *Meet Molly*

When you finish reading each chapter, stop to answer the question.

Chapter 1 What words would you use to describe Molly? List at least four words.

_____

_____

Chapter 2 Imagine that you can give Molly and Ricky advice about teasing. What do you say?

_____

_____

Chapter 3 At the end of the chapter, Molly says she's going to teach Ricky a lesson. What do you predict she'll do and why?

_____

_____

Chapter 4 This chapter is called "War!" Do you think that's a good name for it? Why or why not?

_____

_____

_____

Name _____

After Reading *Meet Molly*

1. Imagine that you are Molly or Ricky. Write Dad a note about your fight and how you feel now that it's over.

_____

_____

_____

_____

2. How is your life like Molly's life? How is your life different from hers? List at least two likenessess and two differences.

Ways My Life Is Like Molly's	Ways My Life Is Different from Molly's
_____	_____
_____	_____
_____	_____
_____	_____

3. Molly wears a locket where she keeps a picture of her father. Draw a person, place, or thing that is important to you. Then write one or two sentences that explain why it is important.

Name _____

After Reading "Looking Back" in *Meet Molly*

1. Citizens in the armed forces and citizens at home did what they could for the war effort. List ways that each group helped win the war. Think about the jobs people did and the changes and sacrifices they made.

People in the Armed Forces	People at Home

2. Would you rather have been in the armed forces or at home during the war? Why?

_____

_____

_____

MOLLY LEARNS ★ A LESSON ★

A SCHOOL STORY

USING THE PICTURE MAP

Before students start to read, point out the Willow Street School and Molly's house and neighborhood, including Alison's house.

VOCABULARY WORDS

See TG page 6 for activities.

cooperating (9): working together
participate (16): take part
complicated (18): difficult
substitutes (23): replacements
mission (30): assignment, job
oath (31): promise

SIMILES AND METAPHORS

Point out the author's use of similes and metaphors throughout this story. On page 1, for example, Miss Campbell's long curls "swung like a dancer's skirt," and Molly compares her own hair to sticks. These figures of speech help make the descriptions vivid.

PLOT SUMMARY

Chapter 1 Molly's morning in Miss Campbell's orderly third-grade class isn't going well. She misses a geography question while daydreaming, feels proud and then sad and afraid when telling the class what Dad is doing in England, and gives the wrong answer in the multiplication bee.

Chapter 2 Miss Campbell announces the Lend-a-Hand Contest. Students will compete with projects to help the war effort. While Molly daydreams about winning the contest, Miss Campbell accepts Alison's suggestion that the girls in the class knit socks—a task Molly thinks will be too hard.

Chapter 3 Molly talks her two best friends, Susan and Linda, into planning their own Lend-a-Hand project. The girls decide to collect bottlecaps for scrap metal. To surprise and impress everyone in school, they decide to keep their project a secret, like top secret agents. When Alison comes over to invite Molly to a knitting bee, the girls hide from her so they can keep their project to themselves.

Chapter 4 Gathering bottletops is harder than Molly and her friends thought it would be. While they're going from house to house asking for bottletops, they decide to spy on Alison's knitting bee. Alison's mother sees them and forces them to join the group. Knitting socks is difficult for the girls. Molly suggests an alternative: knitting simple squares and sewing them together to make a blanket. They form an assembly line, with all the girls participating, and are able to produce a blanket to send to a hospital in England. The whole group decides to collect bottletops, too. By cooperating, the girls complete two prize-winning projects.

THEMES IN THE STORY

Allied effort In the first chapter, Miss Campbell teaches her students about "allies—people who work together for the same goal" (page 9). But Molly wants to stand out, to see her picture in the newspaper and her efforts heralded in a headline (page 17). She thinks knitting socks with the other girls is "a terrible idea" (page 18) and convinces her friends to undertake a separate project. In the end, it's all the girls working together that produces the prize-winning projects—and shows "the true meaning of allied effort" (page 59). Similarly, it's the United States working together with its Allies that produces a victory in the war, a victory no single country by itself could have won.

Secrecy Influenced by the secrecy and spies of wartime, Molly and her friends plan to be top secret agents on a mission to collect bottletops (pages 30-31). They will be just like secret agents in the movies, with matching clothes, codes, and a secret hide-out and handshake (pages 30-31). The girls treat Alison like an enemy agent (pages 32-34), and they unsuccessfully try to spy on her knitting bee (pages 47-49). Finally, when the three girls join the others, Molly admits that "some secrets are a lot more fun when you give them away than when you keep them" (page 58).

"LOOKING BACK" SUMMARY

"Looking Back" describes schooling in Molly's day.

- In 1944, teachers were stricter and classrooms were quieter and more orderly than they usually are today.

- Children studied World War Two in school and learned to be patriotic.

- Many scarce resources, like sugar, metal, and rubber, were rationed during the war.

- School children helped the war effort by holding scrap drives, participating in groups such as the Junior Red Cross and the Scouts, and using their allowances to buy War Stamps.

JAPANESE AMERICANS

During the war, many citizens feared that Japanese Americans might be spies. In 1942, the government forced Japanese Americans into detention camps. Despite this treatment, almost all Japanese Americans remained loyal to the United States. In 1988, the government agreed to compensate those who had been detained for the homes and businesses they lost while they were in the camps.

CODES AND CODE BREAKERS

In the Pacific, Americans discovered some of Japan's vital military plans by breaking its code. At the same time, over 400 Navajo marines were keeping America's secrets. They served as "code talkers," using their language to send and receive Allied messages. So few people could speak the language—only 28 non-Navajos, by one esti-mate—that it served perfectly as a code and was never broken by the Axis countries.

FROM THE AUTHOR

The photograph on page 66 shows Ms. Tripp's friend, Beverly Stevens, holding a blanket she and her classmates knitted in 1944 to send to soldiers. The seed for this story came from Ms. Tripp's friend doing just what Molly does in the story!

Name _____

Before Reading *Molly Learns a Lesson*

Look through *Molly Learns a Lesson*. By looking at the cover, the portraits of Molly's family and friends, the story and pictures, and the pages that come before and after the story, you can learn a lot about the book. Then answer the questions below.

1. *Cooperation* is important in the story. Write a definition of *cooperation* and give an example of what it means.

_____

_____

2. What lessons do you think Molly might learn in the story? Why?

_____

_____

3. The fourth chapter of the book is called "Spies and Allies." What are spies and allies? (Look up *spy* and *ally* in a dictionary if you need to.) Do you think Molly will be a spy or an ally?

_____

_____

Name _____

As You Read *Molly Learns a Lesson*

When you finish reading each chapter, stop to answer the question.

Chapter 1 Miss Campbell tells her students that "School is your war duty. Being a good student is as important as being a good soldier." What do you think this means?

_____

_____

_____

Chapter 2 Why doesn't Molly want to help with Alison's project? Do you think her reasons are good ones? Explain your answer.

_____

_____

_____

Chapter 3 If you'd been with Molly and her friends when Alison came to the garage, what would you have done? Why?

_____

_____

_____

Chapter 4 On page 53, Molly isn't sure she should share her idea about the blanket. What makes her speak up?

_____

_____

_____

Name _____

After Reading *Molly Learns a Lesson*

1. Imagine that you're Alison. You've just found out that Molly has been planning a separate project. What would you say to her?

_____

_____

_____

_____

2. One of the lessons that Molly learns is "that some secrets are a lot more fun when you give them away than when you keep them." Do you agree or disagree? Explain your answer.

_____

_____

_____

_____

3. The girls' blanket is an example of one big thing that was made from smaller things contributed by different people. Draw a picture of a project you've worked on or something you've achieved by working with others.

Name _____

After Reading "Looking Back"
in *Molly Learns a Lesson*

1. Write words or phrases in each box to compare schools in
Molly's time and schools today.

	1944	Today
Methods of getting to school		
Desks		
Subjects studied		
Student projects		

2. List two things that you would like about being in school in
1944 and two things that you wouldn't like about it.

Things I Would Like	**Things I Would Not Like**
_____	_____
_____	_____
_____	_____

MOLLY'S ★ SURPRISE ★

A CHRISTMAS STORY

USING THE PICTURE MAP

Before students start to read, point out Molly's house; Willow Street School, where the Boy Scouts are selling Christmas trees; and church, where the McIntires go for a Christmas Eve service.

VOCABULARY WORDS

See TG page 6 for activities.

elegant (18): attractive
scrawny (24): thin, little
enchanted (32): magical, under a spell
tempting (51): inviting
broadcasting (57): putting on the air, sending out

PLOT SUMMARY

Chapter 1 Christmas is only four days away, and no package has arrived from Dad. Dad loves Christmas, and Molly and the rest of the family miss him terribly. Molly is unhappy about the wartime Christmas in general. She knows the holiday will be simple, with practical presents, and that Jill is right: they must be realistic. Mom says that despite the war and Dad's absence, Christmas can be special—but it will be up to them to make it special.

Chapter 2 Things look worse when Gram and Granpa call to say they have a flat tire and can't come. They were bringing the McIntires a Christmas tree, so this change of plans also leaves them without a tree. Molly, Jill, and Ricky decide to pool their money and buy a tree to surprise Mom and Brad. Molly and Jill tell each other their worst fear: no package from Dad might mean that he's hurt, sick, or lost.

Chapter 3 Jill and Molly go outside to play in the new snow and discover a package from Dad on the front porch. A message on the box says, "Keep hidden until Christmas Day!", but Jill isn't sure they should keep this happy secret from the rest of the family. Molly wants to. In the end, they decide that since Dad wants to surprise everyone, they will keep the box hidden in the garage until Christmas morning.

Chapter 4 It's hard for Molly to keep the secret about Dad's box, but she manages. On Christmas Eve, after the McIntires have gone to church, come home, and gone to bed, Molly and Jill sneak out to the garage, bring Dad's package in the house, and put it under the tree. The next morning, everyone else is surprised to see the box, happy about the gifts Dad has sent, and thrilled about the best surprise of all—hearing Dad's voice on a radio broadcast from England.

THEMES IN THE STORY

Hope Mom tells Molly (page 11) that "it's never wrong to keep hoping for good things to happen, especially at Christmas time. That's what Christmas is all about—hope." Molly in turn hopes that Christmas will bring "wonderful surprises" (page 12). Both Jill and Molly hope that something will come from Dad to prove he's okay (pages 29, 40-41), and all of the McIntires join the nation in hoping that this Christmas will "truly bring peace on earth" (pages 48-49).

Resourcefulness With Dad gone, Mom tells Molly that this year the rest of the McIntires will have to make Christmas surprises for themselves (page 11). In the face of their grandparents' canceled visit, the children use a little ingenuity to buy and decorate a Christmas tree (pages 22-26), and the girls manage to keep everyone else from finding out about the surprise from Dad. Just like other families in the early 1940s, the McIntires learn how to find joy in spite of the shortages, hardships, and uncertainties created by the war.

"LOOKING BACK" SUMMARY

"Looking Back" describes Christmas during World War Two.

- Many families were separated during the holidays because soldiers were fighting overseas and restrictions at home prevented much travel.

- To compensate for food rationing and other shortages, people invented new recipes for treats and created homemade decorations for their trees.

- Gifts were usually practical, but parents tried to give children a few small toys to make Christmas special.

- Despite the war, the spirit of Christmas still made many people happy and renewed hope for "peace on earth."

PRICES IN 1944

In 1941, the Office of Price Administration placed price controls on 90 percent of consumer goods. Without these regulations, the cost of goods would have shot up by as much as 1,000 percent. In 1944, a roll of Lifesavers cost 5¢, a Nancy Drew mystery cost 58¢, and a girl's all-wool cardigan sweater cost $2.49.

"MAY YOUR DAYS BE MERRY AND BRIGHT"

*The song lyrics quoted on page 57 are from the classic tune "White Christmas." Composed by Irving Berlin, the song made its debut in the film **Holiday Inn** in 1942. Later it reappeared as the title song in the 1954 movie **White Christmas**. It has since become the best-selling phonograph record of all time.*

FROM THE AUTHOR

Ms. Tripp observed in doing her research that citizens were proud of the habit of thrift they developed during the war, a habit summed up in the saying, "Use it up, wear it out, make it do, or do without!" She says that the people she talked to expressed a plucky toughness and determination about the time. She wanted Molly to learn self-reliance and resourcefulness because she saw how much these qualities were valued by people who lived through the war.

Name _____

Before Reading *Molly's Surprise*

Look through *Molly's Surprise.* By looking at the cover, the portraits of Molly's family and friends, the story and pictures, and the pages that come before and after the story, you can learn a lot about the book. Then answer the questions below.

1. The first chapter is called "A Different Christmas." Name at least two ways that Christmas during the war might be different from past Christmases for Molly and her family.

_____

_____

2. One of the surprises in this story requires Molly to keep a secret. What do you think that secret might be?

_____

_____

3. Americans remembered their duty to help soldiers and sailors during the holidays. List two things the McIntires and their neighbors might do for soldiers and sailors during Christmas.

_____

_____

4. Part of the joy of any holiday is preparing for it and imagining the fun that will occur. Why might Molly be looking forward to the holidays?

_____

_____

Name _____

As You Read *Molly's Surprise*

When you finish reading each chapter, stop to answer the question.

Chapter 1 Jill tells Molly to be "realistic" about this Christmas. Mom tells Molly that Christmas can still be special. Do you agree with Jill, Mom, or both of them? Explain your answer.

_____

_____

_____

Chapter 2 Molly begins to think it's more fun to surprise others than be surprised herself. What causes Molly to have this new thought? Do you agree with her?

_____

_____

_____

Chapter 3 Do you agree with Molly and Jill's decision to keep the package from Dad a secret? Explain your answer.

_____

_____

_____

Chapter 4 When Molly is older, which surprise from this Christmas do you think she'll remember the most? Why do you think so?

_____

_____

_____

After Reading *Molly's Surprise*

1. What was your favorite part of *Molly's Surprise*? Why did you like it?

_____

_____

_____

2. What makes Christmas happy for Molly's family? What do you enjoy most about your favorite holiday?

_____

_____

_____

3. At the beginning of the story, Molly and Jill aren't getting along very well. By the end, they feel closer to one another. Why do their feelings for one another change?

_____

_____

_____

4. Molly and her family have fun planning surprises for each other. Think of a surprise you have given or would like to give someone else. Draw or write about your surprise.

Name _____

After Reading "Looking Back" in *Molly's Surprise*

1. During the war, people supported the war effort by changing the way they celebrated Christmas. Fill in the chart below with examples from pages 60-65.

What People Did	How It Supported the War Effort

2. Why was it important for people to celebrate Christmas or other holidays during the war, even though times were difficult?

_____

_____

_____

HAPPY BIRTHDAY, ★ MOLLY! ★
A SPRINGTIME STORY

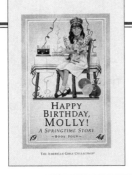

USING THE PICTURE MAP
Before students start to read, point out Molly's house and neighborhood.

VOCABULARY WORDS
See TG page 6 for activities.

shelter (4): safe place
treasured (16): valued, prized
hoity-toity (20): snobbish
rations (20): shares of supplies
allies (48): partners, friends
acquainted (with) (53): familiar with

THE ENGLISH PRINCESSES
When the war began, many Canadians and Americans offered the princesses the safety of their homes. "So kind," wrote the Queen, "but no, there was no question of the royal family taking up their kind offer because the children could not go without me, I could not possibly leave the King and the King would never go."

Princess Elizabeth became Queen Elizabeth II in 1952.

PLOT SUMMARY

Chapter 1 Molly is excited: An English girl is coming to stay with the McIntires to escape the bombing in London. When Emily Bennett arrives, she is pale, thin, and quiet. Molly invites her to play in a make-believe bomb shelter, but Emily doesn't want to. Mom tries to help Molly see how hard the war has been for Emily. She encourages Molly to continue being friendly to Emily even though Emily isn't very friendly to her.

Chapter 2 Molly does her best to befriend Emily, but Emily remains distant. A blackout drill brings the girls closer when Emily describes her scary memories of the Blitz and her guilt about leaving her parents to come to America. Molly reassures Emily that she's done the brave thing. As they talk, the girls realize that they both admire the English princesses, Elizabeth and Margaret Rose.

Chapter 3 Molly and Emily decide to dress in matching outfits, like the English princesses, and walk imaginary dogs. When Mom asks Molly what kind of birthday party she wants, Molly decides to have an English tea party. Since the idea comes from Emily, Molly invites her to help plan the party and to share Molly's birthday.

Chapter 4 Molly frets about the party. Emily says that tea, sandwiches, and lemon tart are served at English teas—not the ice cream and cake Molly wants. Emily also says that they should wear ordinary clothes, not the fancy dresses and crowns Molly envisions. Tension between the two girls erupts in a fight over whose country has given more to the war effort. Molly accuses Emily of ruining her party, and Emily calls Molly a "spoiled child" who cares only about food and clothes.

Chapter 5 The next day, before Molly can apologize to Emily, the rest of the family bursts into their bedroom, shouting birthday greetings. Each girl gets a real puppy, and only then does Emily reveal that her dog in England was killed by a bomb. The two girls realize that the war has been hard on both families, and they make up. Then they follow Mom's suggestion to look in the closet, where they discover matching party dresses!

THEMES IN THE STORY

Compassion Mom tries to help Molly appreciate Emily's feelings (pages 14-15), but Emily's reluctance to talk makes it hard for Molly to understand her (pages 12-13, 16-20). Then, during a blackout, Emily explains what the English have endured during the war (pages 22-26), making the horrors of war real to Molly. Later, Emily realizes that Molly has made sacrifices for the war, too (page 54). War causes universal suffering, and compassion for each other's suffering enables the girls to put aside their differences and become allies once again.

Adaptability As a newcomer, Emily has to adapt to strange American words, foods, and customs (pages 16-17, 20, 28, 30, 40-43). Molly must also adjust to having a visitor in the house and a new friend (pages 12-20). Both girls have learned to adjust to wartime shortages (pages 20, 35, 41-42). After Molly feels she's done most of the adapting for the birthday party, she decides she won't be flexible anymore (page 50). But both girls discover they'd rather adapt and cooperate with each other than be divided (pages 54-56).

"LOOKING BACK" SUMMARY

"Looking Back" describes growing up in Molly's era.

- Most babies were born in hospitals, and conveniences such as canned baby food and washing machines made it easier to take care of babies.

- Vaccinations kept most children healthy.

- Because of the war, some children from other countries were evacuated to the safety of the United States.

- Toys were scarce and expensive, so children invented toys. They also enjoyed comics, movies, and radio.

- People began to see the teen years as a special stage of life. Teens had their own fashions, music, and magazines.

DEFENSE ON THE HOME FRONT

President Roosevelt created the Office of Civilian Defense in May 1941 to coordinate defense programs on the home front. The OCD organized many civilian efforts, including air-raid drills, blackouts, bomb disposal, and aircraft spotting. By late 1943, the threat of enemy attacks had diminished and OCD programs were cut back.

BRITISH WORDS AND PHRASES

*Although Molly and Emily both speak English, they discover they use different words for some things. Emily uses **nurse** for "nanny" and **sister** for "hospital nurse" (page 17), **plimsolls** for "sneakers" (page 20), **tube** for "subway," **mum** for "mom" (page 25), **Girl Guides** for "Girl Scouts" (page 28), and **jumpers** for "sweaters" (page 45). Students can find other British words by asking a librarian for help—or talking to someone from England. Additional examples of British words: **lorry** for "truck," **petrol** for "gasoline," **bonnet** for the "hood" of a car, and **boot** for the "trunk" of a car.*

Name _____

Before Reading *Happy Birthday, Molly!*

Look through *Happy Birthday, Molly!* By looking at the cover, the portraits of Molly's family and friends, the story and pictures, and the pages that come before and after the story, you can learn a lot about the book. Then answer the questions below.

1. In this story, the McIntires have a visitor from England. What would you ask a visitor from England about her country or its customs?

_____

_____

_____

2. From looking at the cover, how do you think birthday celebrations in 1944 were like birthday celebrations today? How do you think they were different?

_____

_____

_____

3. World War Two is going on when Molly turns ten. How do you think the war might make this birthday different for Molly from other birthdays she's had?

_____

_____

_____

Name _____

As You Read *Happy Birthday, Molly!*

When you finish reading each chapter, stop to answer the question.

Chapter 1 Molly can't understand why Emily is so quiet. What might Emily be thinking about on her first day at Molly's home?

_____

_____

Chapter 2 During the blackout drill, Emily tells Molly that Americans don't know how terrible the war is. If you were Molly, would you agree with Emily? Why or why not?

_____

_____

Chapter 3 The author writes, "Spring buds were opening up in the sunshine and Emily was, too" (page 28). What does this mean?

_____

_____

Chapter 4 At the end of this chapter, Molly and Emily get into a fight. If you had been there, what would you have said to help the two of them get along?

_____

_____

Chapter 5 Molly believes her dad would say that "no party was half as important as a friend's feelings." How does Molly show that she thinks people are more important than things?

_____

_____

Name _____

After Reading *Happy Birthday, Molly!*

MOLLY · 1944

18

1. Imagine that you're Molly, Ricky, or Emily. Write a journal entry about what you've learned as a result of Emily's visit to the McIntires.

_____

_____

2. Molly's and Emily's lives are very different, but they also have many things in common. List at least two likenesses and two differences.

How Molly's and Emily's Lives Are Alike	How Molly's and Emily's Lives Are Different
_____	_____
_____	_____
_____	_____
_____	_____

3. In anger, Molly and Emily say mean things to one another. Think of a time when you said something in anger that you didn't mean. How did you feel? What did you do afterward?

_____

_____

4. Molly had a picture in her mind of what Emily would be like. Draw or describe something that turned out to be very different from what you pictured.

32

Name _____

After Reading "Looking Back"
in *Happy Birthday, Molly!*

1. Fill in the chart with examples of ways that growing up is the same today as in 1944.

	In 1944 and Today
Where most babies are born	
What children do in their free time	
Chores children help with	
How children celebrate birthdays	
Things teenagers do	
What young people do when they graduate from high school	

2. If you could choose, would you grow up in Molly's era or today? Give at least two reasons to support your answer.

_____

_____

_____

MOLLY SAVES ★ THE DAY ★

A SUMMER STORY

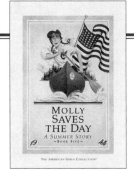

MOLLY
SAVES
THE DAY
A SUMMER STORY
~BOOK FIVE~

THE AMERICAN GIRLS COLLECTION®

HISTORICAL PARALLELS

The Color War parallels World War Two in many ways. In each conflict, two opposing sides are intent on victory. Personal loyalty is often divided between self-protection and the best interests of the group. Participants are pushed beyond their normal limits, often discovering reserves of courage and leadership they didn't know they had. Students can look for other similarities between the two wars.

PLOT SUMMARY

Chapter 1 Three days before summer camp is over, Camp Gowonagin's director announces a Color War. Molly and Susan are assigned to the Blue team and Linda to the Red team. Molly and Susan don't like the idea of the Color War or their bossy team captain, Dorinda. They also dread the thought that the game will require them to face their fears—Molly's of being underwater and Susan's of canoes. Linda, who fears bugs, tells her friends not to take the game too seriously.

Chapter 2 Linda's team, the Reds, paddles to Chocolate Drop Island to plant the flag the Blues must capture. Dorinda outlines the Blue plan. As Molly predicts, the plan fails and the Blues end up in the Red prison on the beach, where Linda is the guard. Because Molly and Susan are delayed when their canoe tips over, they aren't with the other Blues. When they nearly catch up, Linda sends out her teammates to get them. Molly can't believe Linda would betray her and Susan to win the game. Molly sees that the only hope for a Blue victory is to create a new battle plan.

Chapter 3 Molly and Susan implement Molly's new plan. Molly hides in the canoe while Susan paddles to the island. They land away from the beach, and Molly gets out. Susan then paddles to the beach while Molly goes overland, except when she must swim underwater across an inlet. While Susan distracts the Reds, Molly sneaks up behind Linda and dumps worms on her. With Linda and the other Reds caught off guard, Molly frees the prisoners and the Blues paddle back to camp.

Chapter 4 Dorinda is still in the Red prison, so the Blues choose Molly as their new leader. Thinking of the D-Day invasion, Molly suggests that they surprise the Reds by sneaking up on them. The Blues make a floating dock of their canoes at a secret spot known as Poison Point because it's covered with poison ivy. The brave Blues follow Molly through the plants. They capture the Red flag and win the Color War.

Chapter 5 Molly, Susan, and Linda are glad that the war is over and they are no longer enemies. Each has faced a fear—and now all the Blues face a case of poison ivy!

THEMES IN THE STORY

Bravery Before Dad left for the war, he told Molly that "it was okay to be scared because that meant that he had a chance to be brave" (page 16). Just like soldiers, the campers have a chance to be brave—a chance Molly isn't sure she wants (page 17). But in battle, the girls find their courage, just as soldiers do. Susan faces her fear of canoeing (page 38), Molly conquers her fear of swimming underwater (page 40), and Linda copes with worms (page 42).

The nature of war The Color War teaches Molly lessons about war like those learned by soldiers at the front. War creates artificial divisions—teams and armies. Molly observes that "friendship doesn't count during a war" (page 32). War causes the loss of humanity and kindness. As Molly explains, "you can't think of people as people during a war. You think of them as part of an army" (page 35). And war costs so much in human terms that its conclusion gives almost as much cause for celebration as victory does. In the end, Molly thinks no one really won. She's glad they no longer have to choose sides (pages 60-61).

"LOOKING BACK" SUMMARY

"Looking Back" describes going to camp in the 1940s.

- The war made it hard for families to vacation together, so many children went to summer camp on their own.

- Campers learned wilderness skills. Camp counselors planned fun activities.

- In some ways, summer camps were like military camps.

- Children who went to camp often grew up to appreciate and protect the environment.

SLOGANS

Slogans were everywhere during the war, not just at Camp Gowonagin! The Office of War Information, started in 1942, put out slogans on posters and buttons to encourage support for the war. A few examples: "Loose lips sink ships." "Pay your taxes, beat the Axis." "Sow the seeds of Victory: Every garden a munition plant."

THE LANGUAGE OF WAR

*Although Miss Butternut calls the Color War a "game" (page 10), it soon becomes more serious. The campers use military words to talk about it, such as **on the double** (page 19), **oh-nine-hundred** (page 20), and **troops** (page 20). Students can find other examples of military language in the story.*

THE D-DAY INVASION

The D-Day invasion on the beach at Normandy, France, inspired Molly's plan during the Color War (pages 47-52). D-Day was the largest invasion by sea in history. The first day involved almost 5,000 boats and ships, 176,000 men, and over 10,000 airplanes—and cost 10,000 Allied casualties. During the next two weeks, a million Allied troops landed on the beach at Normandy.

Name _____

Before Reading *Molly Saves the Day*

Look through *Molly Saves the Day*. By looking at the cover, the portraits of Molly's family and friends, the story and pictures, and the pages that come before and after the story, you can learn a lot about the book. Then answer the questions below.

1. Where do you think this story takes place? Give reasons to support your answer.

_____

_____

_____

2. In this story, Molly does something brave. What does being brave mean?

_____

_____

_____

3. Chapter 2 in this story is called "We're in the Army Now," and Chapter 5 is called "The Pink Army." What might this story have to do with being in the army?

_____

_____

_____

As You Read *Molly Saves the Day*

When you finish reading each chapter, stop to answer the question.

Chapter 1 Molly isn't sure she likes the idea of the Color War. If you had been with Molly, what would you have said to her?

_____

_____

_____

Chapter 2 Do you think Linda should have blown the whistle on Molly and Susan? Why or why not?

_____

_____

Chapter 3 On page 45, Molly says she feels like she's already lost "something very important." What do you think she's talking about? Do you think she's right?

_____

_____

Chapter 4 Do you think Molly is a good team leader? Why or why not?

_____

_____

Chapter 5 Molly says she doesn't think anybody really won the Color War. Do you agree with her? Why or why not?

_____

_____

Name _____

After Reading *Molly Saves the Day*

MOLLY · 1944

22

1. Imagine that Molly has finished the letter to Dad on page 61. She tells him that she wants to come to camp again. Does she say that she hopes there will be another Color War? Explain why or why not.

_____

_____

2. The Color War is like a real war but different from a real war, too. List at least two likenesses and two differences.

How the Color War and a Real War Are Alike	How the Color War and a Real War Are Different
_____	_____
_____	_____
_____	_____

3. Think about a time when you and a good friend were on opposing teams. Did you feel more loyalty to your team or to your friend? Explain why you felt the way you did.

_____

_____

_____

4. Linda says, "If you can do something you're scared to do, then you're brave" (page 16). Draw or write about a time when you were brave.

Name _____

After Reading "Looking Back"
in *Molly Saves the Day*

1. In the chart below, list things campers did in the 1940s.

	Summer Camps in the 1940s
Learning about health and safety	
Activities	
Pioneer living	
Responsible camp living	
Similarities to army and navy	

2. What would you have liked the most about summer camp in the 1940s? What would you have disliked? Explain your answers.

_____

_____

_____

CHANGES FOR ★ MOLLY ★

A WINTER STORY

USING THE PICTURE MAP

Before students start to read, point out Miss LaVonda's dance studio, Molly's house, the drugstore, and the Veterans' Hospital, where the "Hurray for the U.S.A." show takes place.

VOCABULARY WORDS

See TG page 6 for activities.

veterans (2): retired military people
solo (3): performance by one person
rehearsing (3): practicing
glumly (5): sadly
sophisticated (9): elegant, grown-up
stylish (17): fashionable
mature (33): grown-up

WARTIME FASHION

During the war, the War Production Board prevented fashions from changing—and clothes from becoming obsolete. Regulations kept skirt lengths the same during the war and put off changes in the styles of collars, sleeves, and other elements of clothing design.

PLOT SUMMARY

Chapter 1 Molly and her friends can't wait to dance in the "Hurray for the U.S.A." show. Molly hopes to be chosen for the Miss Victory solo, but fears she won't win the part because of her straight hair. She's tempted to get a permanent wave. Then a letter comes from Dad saying he's coming home—and in time to see the show! Molly is more determined than ever to curl her hair and dance as Miss Victory so she can show Dad how grown-up she is.

Chapter 2 Molly imagines how great it will be to have Dad home and how impressed he'll be with the curly-haired, sophisticated Molly. When Mom finds Molly looking at photo albums, they talk about Dad's return. Mom says that Dad will love Molly no matter what she looks like, but Molly secretly decides to try a perm anyway. Molly gets nervous, though, about Susan's ability to give her the permanent. When Jill offers to set her hair every night instead, Molly gladly agrees.

Chapter 3 Jill keeps her promise, and every night she sets Molly's hair. Molly has trouble sleeping on the pins, but they do produce curls. Unfortunately, the curls come out whenever Molly dances. After experimenting, the girls discover that setting Molly's hair when it's wet solves even this problem. At the end of the week, with her curly "new" hair, Molly wins the part of Miss Victory.

Chapter 4 A week before the show, Mom says that Molly feels feverish and can't keep going to bed with wet hair, so Molly goes back to braids. Mom does let Molly set her hair for the dress rehearsal, where Molly steals the show. But the next day, Molly is too sick to dance. She yanks out her pin curls and braids her hair. While the rest of the family goes to the show, Molly stays home in bed, feeling sorry for herself. But then Dad comes home earlier than expected, and Molly is the only one there to greet him. Dad says Molly looks just as he remembers—perfect!

THEMES IN THE STORY

Change For Molly and her family, war causes many changes, just as it did for the nation. Mom says that war changes people on the inside and the outside (page 18). Molly knows how much Jill has changed (page 31), and Jill reminds Molly of all the ways Molly has changed (pages 32-33). Even Mom has changed, confidently making a speech she would have been too shy to deliver before the war (page 46). After Molly changes herself into the perfect Miss Victory (page 47), she's disappointed by having to return to the "same dumb me" (page 55). But she also realizes that her curls aren't very important (page 56). Molly is older and changed by her experience, just as the nation was older and changed by the experience of the war.

Character vs. appearance Molly is sure that having curly hair will make a big difference in her life—it will help her get the part of Miss Victory (page 7) and prove to Dad that she's grown-up (page 12). Mom says that Dad might look different when he gets home, but he'll still be the "same old Dad at heart." He'll be so happy to see Molly that he won't care how she looks (page 18). Jill says that while Molly may look the same, she's grown up on the inside (pages 32-33). After Molly gets sick and can't be in the show, she sees that her hair didn't matter very much (page 56). When Dad returns, he confirms that what is lovable about someone doesn't change as she grows up and certainly not as her appearance changes (page 58).

"LOOKING BACK" SUMMARY

"Looking Back" describes changes in American life after World War Two.

• People were happy when the war ended, and they believed that the world would be a better place.

• Most Americans' lives returned to normal. People could buy once-scarce items; men took over their old jobs.

• Many people started families and moved to the suburbs. They went into cities only to work and shop.

• America took a leading role in the effort to rebuild its allies and enemies.

• The United States dropped the first atomic bomb during the war. After the war, the United Nations was formed to prevent wars.

THE ENORMOUS COST OF THE WAR

A total of 16,112,566 Americans fought in World War Two. About 2.5 percent were killed (405,399); another 4 percent were wounded (670,846).

In Molly's world, Miss Campbell's fiancé is killed (page 20), Grace Littlefield's father is disabled (page 20), and Dad misses years of his children's growing up (page 32). Although the war ends, its effects never end for some families (pages 21-22).

HAIRSTYLES DURING THE WAR

Women were encouraged during the war to have their hair cut short. Hairpins for styling long hair were in short supply, and long hair was hazardous for women working in factories. Among the recommended hairstyles were the Victory Roll and the Liberty Cut.

WOMEN AND WORK

After the war, some women willingly gave up their wartime jobs. But most were forced out of their "men's" jobs by a combination of union, management, and governmental practices. Even though the war had only temporarily enlarged the sphere of work available to women, it permanently increased the number of working women. By the early 1950s, more women were working outside the home than at any time during the war.

Name _____

Before Reading *Changes for Molly*

Look through *Changes for Molly*. By looking at the cover, the portraits of Molly's family and friends, the story and pictures, and the pages that come before and after the story, you can learn a lot about the book.

1. The title of the book is *Changes for Molly*. What changes do you think might take place for Molly?

_____

_____

_____

2. In this story, people change in ways you can see and in ways you can't see. Give an example of each kind of change.

_____

_____

_____

3. In this story, Molly wants to look sophisticated and grown-up. Describe how you think a sophisticated person looks and acts.

_____

_____

_____

Name _____

As You Read *Changes for Molly*

When you finish reading each chapter, stop to answer the question.

Chapter 1 Molly has a plan: She'll get a permanent, win the part of Miss Victory—and show Dad how grown-up she is. Do you think her plan will work? Give reasons for your answer.

_____

_____

Chapter 2 If you could give Molly advice about whether to change her appearance, what would you say?

_____

_____

Chapter 3 Molly makes several sacrifices to be Miss Victory. Do you think winning the solo part is worth the effort she goes to? Why or why not?

_____

_____

Chapter 4 Molly is disappointed that she's too sick to dance in the show. If you had been with Molly, what would you have said to help her feel better?

_____

_____

After Reading *Changes for Molly*

26

1. Imagine that you are Molly and you have Dad all to yourself until everyone else comes home from the show. What do you want to tell him?

_____

_____

_____

_____

2. What is the most important change that Molly makes in this story? What is the most important change that happens in her family? Explain your answers.

_____

_____

_____

_____

3. Think about the changes in your life during the last year. Draw or write about the most important change.

Name _____

After Reading "Looking Back" in *Changes for Molly*

MOLLY · 1944

27

1. For each of the following areas of life in America, list at least two changes that occurred after World War Two.

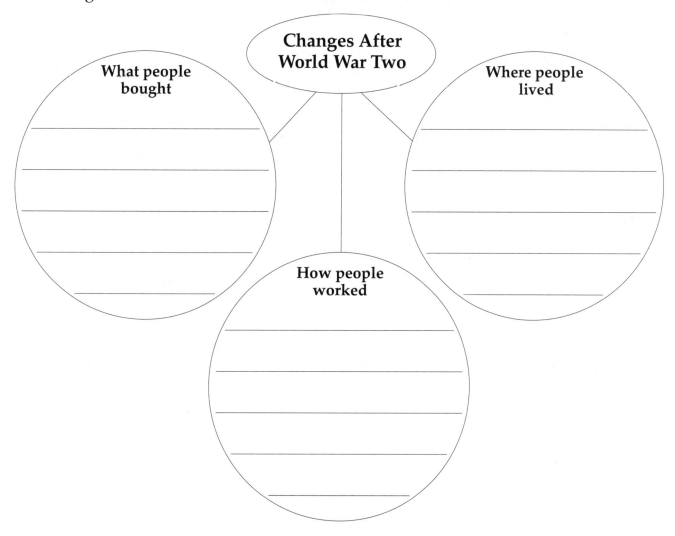

Changes After World War Two

What people bought

Where people lived

How people worked

2. After World War Two, many countries joined together to create the United Nations in hopes of preventing war. List at least two ideas you have for creating a more peaceful world.

_____

_____

_____

_____

HANDS-ON
★ HISTORY ★

OTHER PROJECTS

- *Write letters between a World War Two soldier and his family.*

- *Assemble a recipe book for ration-free foods or Victory garden dishes.*

- *Play a classroom version of Color War and discuss the experience.*

- *Put on a "Hurray for the U.S.A." show.*

- *Write a story outline or another chapter describing what happens to Molly and her family now that Dad is home.*

- *Give a speech as President Roosevelt or another world leader from the 1940s.*

- *Find out what was going on in another country in the world in 1944.*

- *Create a glossary of British words and phrases. The side note on TG page 29 lists a few words students could begin with.*

- *Plant a Victory garden in the classroom.*

Call
VEGETABLES
INTO SERVICE

PROJECTS FOR STUDENTS

This section has blackline masters to help students do five projects:

- Give a tour of Molly's hometown (TG page 47).
- Interview Molly (TG page 50).
- Present a radio program (TG page 52).
- Create a display of their community during World War Two (TG page 55).
- Produce a World War Two issue of Molly's hometown newspaper, *The Jefferson Daily News* (TG page 58).

The projects tap a diversity of student talents and interests, from listening and speaking to conducting research to using skills in art and writing.

The blackline masters function as checklists for students. The amount of direction students will need in addition to the checklists will vary greatly, depending on the students themselves and their ambition. It's possible to do the projects quite simply or to make them long-term, in-depth undertakings.

Students will find it helpful—and maybe inspiring—to study real-world products that resemble their projects. For example, students who are planning a tour of Molly's hometown can contact historical societies or travel agents to get sample tour brochures. Students presenting a radio program could visit a local radio station. Students who are preparing the newspaper can examine a real newspaper and talk to local journalists.

Name _____

Give a Tour of Molly's Hometown

Molly lived in Jefferson, Illinois, her whole life. She knew her way around the town very well. But visitors like Emily Bennett would need help getting to know the town. Use the picture map, "Molly's World," to plan a tour to help visitors. Visitors can take the tour by following the map.

1. Decide how visitors will take the tour. You can give the tour in many ways. Choose one or more of the methods below, or write your own idea.

☐ A list of places you recommend visiting

☐ An audiotape that people listen to as they take the tour

☐ A brochure with descriptions and pictures of places in Jefferson

☐ A script to use as you lead visitors on the tour

☐ Your idea: _____

2. Gather information. You can find information to plan the tour on the picture map itself and in the six books about Molly. A librarian can probably help you find other sources of information about towns in the Midwest during World War Two. For example, you could learn about the kinds of trees or buildings that were common. Write down the sources you use.

☐ The books about Molly. Titles: _____

_____

☐ Other books. Titles and authors: _____

_____

_____

☐ Other sources (videos, CD-ROMs, and so on): _____

_____

Continued on blackline master 29.

Name _____

Give a Tour of Molly's Hometown   *Continued*

3. Plan the tour. Decide on four more places to include on the tour. One place is already listed. Choose places that would be interesting to your visitors. Use a chart like this to make your plans.

Place	Why It's Interesting
1. Movie theater	Movies were important during the war. Newsreels provided information about the war, and movies distracted people from their worries.
2.	
3.	
4.	
5.	

Continued on blackline master 30.

48

Name _____

Give a Tour of Molly's Hometown   *Continued*

4. Create your tour materials. Make the list, tape, brochure, script, or other tour materials you've decided on. Before you let visitors take the tour, ask a student or your teacher to review the materials and suggest improvements.

5. Plan an evaluation. Decide on questions to ask yourself when you finish the tour. Select two visitors to evaluate the tour, too. Have them write answers to the questions below or tell you their answers. Start with these questions. Add your own questions to the list.

• Was the tour easy to follow?

• Was it clear why places were interesting?

• What place seemed most interesting?

• How could the tour be improved?

6. Have visitors take the tour! Remember to evaluate the tour yourself and have visitors evaluate it, too.

Name _____

Interview Molly

If you've read one or more of the books about Molly, you know a lot about her. You can use what you know to conduct an interview with her, like the kind you've probably seen on TV. You'll need to work with at least one other student. You can make plans together. Then, during the interview, one of you will take Molly's part and the other will ask questions.

1. Decide on your audience. Here are some possible audience members. Put a check next to people who will hear the interview. Remember to keep your audience in mind as you plan your interview.

☐ Classmates   ☐ Younger students

☐ Your family   ☐ Older students

☐ Other people: _____

2. Decide what kind of interview you will conduct. You can conduct an interview in many ways. Check the method you want to use.

☐ Audiotape   ☐ Interview in front of

☐ Videotape   a live audience

☐ Other method: _____

3. Plan your questions and answers. Some possible questions are listed below. Add others you'd like to use. Jot down your questions on 3- x 5-inch cards. Write notes for answers on other cards. Don't try to write down exactly what you'll say. The interview should sound like a conversation, so you'll just want to glance at your cards, not read them.

• How old are you?

• When were you born?

• Who are your family members? What are they like?

• Who are your best friends? How would you describe them?

• How does World War Two affect you?

• What is the biggest change the war has made in your life? Why is that change so significant?

Continued on blackline master 32.

Name  _____

Interview Molly   *Continued*

4. Make a checklist of things to do before the interview.
A checklist helps you remember everything you need to do.
Here's a start. Add other things you think of. Review your list
to make sure it's complete, and then ask your teacher to check
it, too.

☐ Set a date for the interview.

☐ Decide where the interview will take place. If you're going
   to have a live audience, invite them.

☐ Arrange for any help you need, such as someone to run a
   tape recorder or video camera.

☐ Arrange for any equipment you need.

☐ Gather any props you want to use, such as a microphone,
   pictures of Molly and her family, or costumes.

☐ Decide who will be Molly and who will ask questions.

5. Plan an evaluation. Decide on questions to ask yourself
after you finish the interview. Select two people who hear the
interview to evaluate it, too. Have them write answers to the
questions below or tell you their answers. Start with these
questions. Add your own questions to the list.

• Did the interview give information about life during World
  War Two?

• Was it easy to understand the questions and answers?

• Did the interview sound natural—like a conversation?

• How could the interview be improved?

6. Rehearse. Go through the interview once or twice so you
know how it will go. But don't rehearse more than that. You
want the interview to sound natural, not like something you've
memorized.

7. Present the interview.

8. Evaluate the interview. Use the questions in step 5, and
have the two people you've selected use the questions, too.

Name _____

Present a Radio Program

From reading the books about Molly, you know that the radio was very important in the 1940s. Most people did not have televisions, but almost every family had a radio. They listened to the news, speeches, dramas, comedies, and musical programs on the radio. You can plan and present a radio program like one Molly heard. You will probably want to work on this project with at least one other student.

1. Decide on your audience. Put a check next to people who will hear your radio program. Remember to keep your audience in mind as you plan your program.

☐ Classmates   ☐ Younger students

☐ Your family   ☐ Older students

☐ Other people: _____

2. Decide what kind of radio program you will have. You can do different kinds of programs. Check the kind you want to do.

☐ Comedy   ☐ Music concert

☐ Drama   ☐ News

☐ Western   ☐ Speech (such as a presidential "fireside chat")

☐ Mystery

☐ Other idea: _____

3. Gather information. The kind of information you'll need will depend on what kind of program you have. A librarian can probably help you find useful sources, including tapes of radio programs from the 1940s. Write down the sources you use.

☐ Books. Titles and authors: _____

_____

☐ Other sources (audiotapes, videos, CD-ROMs, and so on):

_____

_____

Continued on blackline master 34.

Name _____

Present a Radio Program   *Continued*

4. Plan the program. Your program could have one person talking about a topic. Or it could involve a whole cast of people reading from a script. You might include musical recordings or sound effects. Put a check next to what you will need for your program. You could check just one thing or more than one thing.

☐ Reporter or announcer

☐ Music

☐ Sound effects

☐ Commercials

☐ A cast of performers

☐ A script

☐ Other things: _____

---

5. Make a checklist of things to do before your program.
A checklist helps you remember everything you need to do. Here's a start. Add other things you think of. Review your list to make sure it's complete, and then ask your teacher to check it.

☐ Set a date for your broadcast.

☐ Decide where the radio broadcast will take place. If you're going to have a live audience, invite them.

☐ Arrange for any help you need, such as someone to run a tape recorder.

☐ Arrange for any equipment you need.

☐ Gather any props you want to use, such as a microphone or supplies for sound effects.

☐ Write a script, if necessary, and arrange time to practice.

☐ Decide who will play which parts in the program.

☐ Have everyone prepare the part he or she will have.

Continued on blackline master 35.

Name _____

MOLLY · 1944

35

Present a Radio Program   *Continued*

6. Plan an evaluation. Decide on questions to ask yourself after you finish the program. Select two other people to evaluate the program, too. Have them write answers to the questions below or tell you their answers. Start with these questions. Add your own questions to the list.

• Did the radio program clearly inform or entertain (depending on the type of program)?

• Did the program sound like a radio broadcast from the 1940s?

• Was the program easy to understand?

7. Rehearse. Go through the program once or twice so you know how it will go. Don't memorize the program, but be familiar with what you are going to say and do before the broadcast.

8. Present your program. Remember to evaluate the program when you're done and have others evaluate it, too.

Name _____

Make a Display About Your Community During World War Two

Many people remember living through World War Two. You can use what you know about the war and the resources in your own community to plan a display showing what your town or neighborhood was like in Molly's time. You can make a display by yourself or work together with classmates.

1. Gather information. Begin planning your display by talking to people and reading about and looking at pictures of your community during World War Two. Talk to your teacher, a librarian, your older relatives, or visit a local historical society or museum to locate books, old newspapers, and pictures. Write down the sources you use.

☐ Books. Titles and authors: _____

_____

☐ Old newspapers. Titles and dates: _____

_____

☐ People: _____

_____

☐ Other resources: _____

_____

2. Decide what you want your display to show. Your display could focus on the people in your community who served in the armed forces during the war. It could highlight local activities related to the war or what it was like to be a young person in your community. It could be about just one part of the war, or it could be a collection of many things about it. Write what you want your display to show.

_____

Continued on blackline master 37.

Name _____

Make a Display *Continued*

3. Plan what you will make or collect for your display. Here are some ideas for the display. Choose one or more of these ideas or think of your own.

☐ Pictures and photographs

☐ Artifacts, like ration books or war medals, with labels explaining them

☐ Audiotapes of interviews you've done with people who lived during World War Two

☐ Recordings of old radio programs

☐ Posters

☐ A timeline

☐ Clothing, toys, and other items used in the early 1940s

☐ Newspapers or magazines from the early 1940s

☐ A videotape showing local buildings from the early 1940s

☐ A brochure explaining the display

☐ Other ideas: _____

4. Decide when and where to show your display. Talk to your teacher, librarian, or principal to identify a good place. You may want to set up the display in the classroom, the school library, or a local museum or store window.

5. Plan an evaluation. Decide on questions to ask yourself when you finish the display. Select two other people to evaluate the display, too. Have them write answers to the questions below or tell you their answers. Start with these questions. Add your own questions to the list.

• Does the display express important and accurate information about your community during World War Two?

• What is the most interesting thing about the display?

• How could the display be improved?

Continued on blackline master 38.

Make a Display *Continued*

6. Gather materials and make your display. Keep a list of anything you borrow so you can return it when you're done. Make signs and labels so viewers will understand what's in the display. Be sure to protect your work area if you are using paints, glue, or similar materials.

7. Present your display. Show your display to your teacher, classmates, family members, or other people. Remember to evaluate your work and have others evaluate it, too. When you've finished the project, write thank-you notes to the people who helped you.

Name _____

Produce *The Jefferson Daily News*

From reading the books about Molly, you know a lot about what life was like during World War Two. You can use what you know to create a newspaper or part of a newspaper from Molly's hometown in 1944. You could make the newspaper by yourself or work together with some of your classmates.

1. Decide what will be in your newspaper. Look through a real newspaper to see what kinds of articles and other information it has. Then decide what your newspaper will include. Put a check next to those items.

☐ World news

☐ National news

☐ Local news, including school and club news

☐ Editorials

☐ Obituaries

☐ Schedule of local events

☐ Weather forecast

☐ Recipes

☐ Household advice

☐ Book and movie reviews

☐ Advertisements and classifieds

☐ Comics

☐ Other ideas: _____

2. Plan your newspaper. Decide who will be responsible for writing each item, what it will be about, and where it will go in the paper. What will go on the front page? How much space will each item take? Also decide when each article is due so that the paper can be assembled.

Continued on blackline master 40.

Name _____

Produce *The Jefferson Daily News*   *Continued*

3. Plan an evaluation. Write questions you can ask yourself after you've written the newspaper. Here are possible questions to use. Add other questions you think of.

• Do the articles seem like they were written during World War Two?

• Do the articles give accurate details about life during World War Two?

• Are the articles easy to read?

• Does the newspaper look like a real newspaper?

4. Write the articles. Just like a real reporter, you will have to research the information for each article. Use the books about Molly, encyclopedias, and other resources to help you. Try to use information from the Molly books whenever possible. Sometimes you might have to make things up, such as a name or a date. For example, suppose you decide to write an obituary for Miss Campbell's boyfriend. You can make up his name but you can say he died in one of the actual battles of World War Two, such as the D-Day invasion in Normandy, France.

5. Revise the articles. Look over the questions you listed in step 3. Make revisions to improve the articles and other parts of the newspaper.

6. Assemble and display the newspaper. After all the articles and other items are done, put them together to make the newspaper. You can do this on a computer, or you can paste all of the articles on large sheets of paper. Don't forget to write headlines. Then make copies of your paper to give to readers. Or display the original copy on a bulletin board or in some other location that makes it easy for others to read.

7. Evaluate your newspaper. Have readers evaluate it, too, using the questions in step 3. Readers can write their evaluations or tell you their thoughts.

RESPONSE KEY

Blackline Master 2, TG page 8
1. Responses will vary.
2. Willow Street, Adams Avenue, and Oak Street
3. Responses will vary.
4. West

Blackline Master 3, TG page 9
5. *Ways Molly's Classroom is Like Mine:* Responses will vary, but students may list physical features that their classroom has in common with Molly's, such as the blackboard, map, globe, flag, seats that are attached to desks, posters on the wall or bulletin board, and so on. *Ways Molly's Classroom Is Different from Mine:* Responses will vary, but students may mention that they don't have posters for bonds in their classrooms, that their desks look different from Molly's, and that they don't have practices in their room for enemy attacks.
6. The old form of transportation is a horse-drawn vehicle. Horse-drawn vehicles were sometimes used during the war because gasoline was in short supply.
7. Possibilities include the women making bandages at the Red Cross, the practice for enemy attack taking place in Molly's classroom, the scrap drive taking place at the movie theater, the soldiers at the railroad station, the women working at the airplane factory, the signs to buy bonds in Molly's classroom and at the railroad station, the horse-drawn vehicle, and the Victory garden in Molly's yard and in other people's yards.
8. Responses will vary.

Meet Molly

Blackline Master 4, TG page 12
1. Responses will vary.
2. Possible responses: She's a friendly girl who likes to dress up and have fun. She's mischievous and seems to get into humorous predicaments, such as those shown on pages 34 and 47.
3. Students might mention "getting even" or "getting back at someone."
4. Responses will vary.

Blackline Master 5, TG page 13
1. Possible responses: grumpy, stubborn, lonely (for her father), loving, grateful.
2. Responses will vary.
3. Predictions and reasons will vary.
4. Students might agree that it is a good chapter title because it accurately describes the conflict that erupts as Molly and Ricky launch attacks on each other. Students might disagree because the war between Molly and Ricky is really just teasing and not like the anger and hatred that fuel a real war. Also, no one is wounded or killed in this war.

Blackline Master 6, TG page 14
1. Responses will vary.
2. Students might make their comparisons based on age, family, interests, appearance, or experiences.
3. Responses will vary.

Blackline Master 7, TG page 15
1. Suggested responses follow.
People in the Armed Forces: Became soldiers, pilots, and sailors. Drove ambulances, jeeps, and tanks. Worked in military hospitals and offices. Ordered supplies and nursed the wounded.
People at Home: Hung stars in their windows to show support for soldiers. Used less gasoline and metal. Planted Victory gardens to raise their own food. Volunteered to knit socks, make bandages, and pack boxes of food. Worked for the Red Cross and organized blood drives. Car factories switched to making planes and tanks. Clothing factories made uniforms and tents. Shoe factories made marching boots. Toy factories made war equipment. Women went to work in offices and factories.
2. Responses will vary.

Molly Learns a Lesson

Blackline Master 8, TG page 18
1. Students might mention "working together" or "being part of a team where members help each other." Examples will vary.
2. Possible responses: Molly might learn school lessons, because the cover says it's a school story. Maybe she will have knitting lessons, based on the illustrations on pages 35 and 56.
3. A *spy* secretly watches an enemy or steals enemy secrets. An *ally* cooperates with others to work toward a common goal. Responses to the second question will vary.

Blackline Master 9, TG page 19
1. Students might mention that everyone on the home front is expected to work hard so that soldiers can concentrate on winning the war. If students are good in school, they are freeing their parents to spend more time supporting the war effort.
2. Molly wants her project to be the best so she will get special attention from Miss Campbell. She also knows that it's hard to knit socks. Responses to the second question and explanations will vary.
3. Responses will vary.
4. When Grace Littlefield begins to cry over the frustration of knitting socks, Molly feels sorry for her. She shares her idea about the blanket because it's an easier project that the girls could complete successfully.

Blackline Master 10, TG page 20
1. Responses will vary.
2. Students might agree that surprising someone else with a secret is worth giving it away. Students might disagree, because part of the fun of a secret is the feeling you get from knowing something no one else does.
3. Responses will vary.

Blackline Master 11, TG page 21

1. Responses in the second column will vary. Responses for the "1944" column follow.

Methods of getting to school: Walking, riding bikes.

Desks: Fastened to floor in straight rows.

Subjects studied: Reading, spelling, arithmetic, geography, World War Two.

Student projects: Wrote letters to pen pals; held scrap drives and contests; made food packages for soldiers; rolled bandages; knit sweaters, socks, and blankets.

2. Responses will vary.

Molly's Surprise

Blackline Master 12, TG page 24

1. Students might mention that Christmas will be different because of Dad's absence, the likelihood of getting more practical gifts, and a shortage of the usual holiday sweets.

2. Responses will vary.

3. Students might mention writing letters, sending cards and gift packages, and inviting home-front soldiers to share holiday meals.

4. Students might mention that Molly is anticipating hearing from Dad, having school vacation, getting gifts, and enjoying seasonal events such as church programs and radio specials.

Blackline Master 13, TG page 25

1. Students might agree with Jill because if Molly expects too much, she's sure to be disappointed since supplies are scarce and Dad won't be there. Students might agree with Mom because if Molly takes a negative attitude, she'll be too glum to enjoy any part of the holiday and there's bound to be something she can enjoy.

2. Seeing Mom's delight at the Christmas tree makes Molly take joy in surprising others. Responses will vary to the second question.

3. Students might argue that Molly and Jill should keep the package a secret because that's what Dad wanted, and the gifts will be more special if they are a surprise. Others might argue that they shouldn't keep the package a secret because the family is worried about Dad and would be reassured to know he's safe.

4. Responses will vary.

Blackline Master 14, TG page 26

1. Responses will vary.

2. Students might mention that Christmas was happy for Molly's family because Dad was safe, he sent a radio message and gifts, they all did something to make the holiday happier, and they could enjoy simple pleasures such as the snow and the church program. Responses to the second question will vary.

3. Possible response: Jill and Molly become closer because they share their worst fear—that Dad isn't safe—and the secret of the package from Dad.

4. Responses will vary.

Blackline Master 15, TG page 27

1. Four possible sets of responses follow.

• People who lived near training camps invited soldiers and sailors to their homes for Christmas. This helped people in the armed forces feel less lonely.

• People didn't take unnecessary trips or travel much by bus or train. This saved gas and other resources for the war effort.

• Home-front cooks made up recipes for treats with less butter and sugar. This saved rationed supplies.

• People came up with new ways to decorate their Christmas trees. This saved metal, paper, and other resources for the war effort.

2. Holidays gave people an escape from work and worry. They also reminded them of the reason the war was being fought: to bring peace on earth and goodwill to all.

Happy Birthday, Molly!

Blackline Master 16, TG page 30

1. Responses will vary.

2. Responses will vary.

3. Possible responses: Dad will miss Molly's birthday. She won't be able to have many sweet treats. She might not get many gifts. Because of her Red Cross work, Mom won't have much time to help plan a party.

Blackline Master 17, TG page 31

1. Possible responses: Emily might be thinking how she misses and worries about her parents. She might be wondering if Molly and the McIntires will like her. She might be thinking about how strange America is.

2. Students might agree because American homes aren't being bombed and civilians aren't being killed. Students might disagree because many Americans are fighting and dying and Americans at home are making sacrifices for the war.

3. Emily is friendlier and more relaxed.

4. Responses will vary.

5. Molly apologizes to Emily and renews her enthusiasm for the birthday party.

Blackline Master 18, TG page 32

1. Responses will vary.

2. Suggested responses follow.

How Molly's and Emily's Lives Are Alike: Both girls are separated from at least one parent because of the war. Both have been forced to give up things they like, such as toys and sweets, because of the war.

How Molly's and Emily's Lives Are Different: Molly lives in her own house; Emily doesn't. Molly has only heard about the war, but Emily has experienced it.

3. Responses will vary.

4. Responses will vary.

Blackline Master 19, TG page 33

1. Suggested responses follow.

Where most babies are born: In the hospital.

What children do in their free time: Play games, go to the movies, read books.

Chores children help with: Making beds, doing dishes, taking out the garbage.

How children celebrate birthdays: Have parties with treats and games.

Things teenagers do: Wear their own fashions, listen to music, read magazines, "hang out" together, drive, date.

What young people do when they graduate from high school: Go to college, go to work, get married, or all three.

2. Responses will vary.

Molly Saves the Day

Blackline Master 20, TG page 36
1. The story probably takes place in an outdoor setting because the cover shows Molly in a boat with woods in the background. The boat has a camp logo on it, and Molly is wearing what could be a uniform, so the story might take place at a wilderness camp.
2. Students' responses should express the idea that being brave means having courage or overcoming fear.
3. Students might suggest that Molly is in a camp that is sponsored by the army, or that there are things about camp that are like the army, or that there is some kind of battle at camp that is like a war.

Blackline Master 21, TG page 37
1. Responses will vary.
2. Responses will vary.
3. Molly has lost the trust and support she's always shared with her friends. She and Linda "attacked" each other for the sake of their teams. Responses will vary to the second question.
4. Students might think Molly is a good leader because she comes up with a clever plan that succeeds. When the plan calls for a sacrifice (going through the poison ivy), Molly doesn't ask her team to do anything she isn't willing to do. Students might think Molly isn't a good team leader because she forces the Blue team to crawl through poison ivy.
5. Students might agree because although Molly's team wins the war, the victory comes at the cost of personal loyalties. Students might disagree because the Blues capture the Red flag fair and square.

Blackline Master 22, TG page 38
1. Responses will vary.
2. Suggested responses follow.
How the Color War and a Real War Are Alike: There are two opposing sides. People must be brave in order to win. Some people are taken prisoner. The leaders plot "battle" strategy. People are injured (with poison ivy).
How the Color War and a Real War Are Different: In the Color War, there are no weapons, people don't die, and everyone knows it's just for fun.
3. Responses will vary.
4. Responses will vary.

Blackline Master 23, TG page 39
1. Suggested responses follow.
Learning about health and safety: First aid, water safety, good nutrition.
Activities: Horseback riding, swimming, arts and crafts.
Pioneer living: Cooking over an open fire, building a shelter with a blanket and sticks, identifying animal tracks and plants.
Responsible camp living: Cleaning cabins, making beds, gathering firewood.
Similarities to army and navy: Living in a group, daily inspections, words from the military.
2. Responses will vary.

Changes for Molly

Blackline Master 24, TG page 42
1. Students might predict that these changes will take place: Dad will come home, Molly and her friends will be in a show, Molly will change her hairstyle, Molly will get sick.
2. Responses will vary.
3. Responses will vary.

Blackline Master 25, TG page 43
1. Students might predict the plan won't work because Molly's permanent will make her hair look worse. She might not get the part of Miss Victory. Dad might not make it home in time for the show. She might make a mistake during the show and be disappointed in her performance. Others may predict that Molly's plan will work because she's very determined.
2. Students might say they would agree with Mom and point out that what's important is not how a person looks but how he or she acts and feels. Or students might argue that Molly should be encouraged to change her looks to achieve her goal.
3. Students might say yes, because Molly wouldn't have had the same confidence and enthusiasm when she danced if she didn't have curly hair. Students might say no, because Molly was the best dancer and probably would have gotten the part anyway.
4. Responses will vary.

Blackline Master 26, TG page 44
1. Responses will vary.
2. Possibilities for Molly's most important change: She learns that looks aren't everything; she sees that she's grown-up on the inside. Possibilities for the most important change in the family: Dad finally comes home from the war; Jill and Molly grow closer.
3. Responses will vary.

Blackline Master 27, TG page 45
1. *What people bought:* It was easier to buy household products. Televisions were popular things to buy.
Where people lived: Many families moved to the new suburbs that were built outside cities. Many people lived in prefab houses. People sometimes moved far away from their old neighborhoods in order to have their own homes.
How people worked: Most women gave their wartime jobs back to men. Women were told it was important for them to work at home. People from the suburbs commuted to work in the cities.
2. Responses will vary.

BOOKS ABOUT WORLD WAR TWO

Fiction

Barrie, Barbara. *Lone Star.* Delacorte, 1990; Dell, 1992. In this story set in 1944, Jane must cope with being transplanted from her Jewish community in Chicago to Texas. Challenging.

Bishop, Claire H. *Twenty and Ten.* Puffin, 1978. Ten Jewish children take refuge with other French schoolchildren during World War Two. Average.

Chaikin, Miriam. *Friends Forever.* Harper & Row, 1988. Molly and her friends deal with school troubles, fear of World War Two, and first dates during their sixth-grade year. One of a series about this character. Average.

Choi, Sook Nyul. *Year of Impossible Goodbyes.* Houghton Mifflin, 1991. After Sookan and her family survive the Japanese occupation of their northern Korean community during World War Two, they face new dangers when Korea is divided at the 38th Parallel. Challenging.

Delton, Judy. *Kitty in the Middle.* Houghton Mifflin, 1979. Episodic adventures of three fourth-grade girls who attend a parochial school during World War Two. Average.

Estes, Eleanor. *The Hundred Dresses.* Harcourt, 1944, 1974. A Polish immigrant girl is teased by classmates who later learn a lesson about tolerance and acceptance. Average.

Frascino, Edward. *Eddie Spaghetti.* Harper & Row, 1978. The everyday adventures and predicaments of a nine-year-old boy in New York City during the 1940s. Some readers might object to the parents in the story hitting their children as punishment. Average.

Garrigue, Sheila. *All the Children Were Sent Away.* Bradbury, 1976. An eight-year-old girl evacuated from England experiences many adventures on her way to Canada. Challenging.

Green, Connie Jordan. *The War at Home.* Margaret K. McElderry, 1989. Mattie puzzles over her father's secret job in Oak Ridge, Tennessee, and her father's affection for Mattie's infuriating cousin, Virgil. Challenging.

Hahn, Mary D. *Stepping on the Cracks.* Clarion, 1991; Avon, 1993. Elizabeth copes with concerns about her older brother, who is battling on the frontlines, and the school bully, who is fighting a tyrant of another sort. Challenging.

Hest, Amy. *Love You, Soldier.* Four Winds Press, 1991; Puffin, 1993. A moving story of a young girl whose family undergoes many changes during World War Two. Easy.

Holm, Anne. *North to Freedom.* Harcourt, 1965, 1990. After escaping from a concentration camp where he has spent most of his life, a twelve-year-old boy tries to cope with an entirely strange world as he flees north to freedom in Denmark. Challenging.

Hoobler, Dorothy, and Thomas Hoobler. *Aloha Means Come Back: The Story of a World War II Girl.* Silver Burdett, 1991. Two girls, one Anglo and one of Japanese ancestry, are separated and united by tumultuous events at Pearl Harbor in 1941. Average.

Kudlinski, Kathleen V. *Pearl Harbor Is Burning: A Story of World War II.* Viking, 1991. A boy and his new Japanese friend witness the bombing of Pearl Harbor in 1941. Based on a true account. Average.

Laird, Christa. *Shadow of the Wall.* Greenwillow, 1989. Young Misha struggles to help his family survive the Nazi clampdown on the Warsaw Ghetto. Challenging.

Little, Jean. *Listen for the Singing.* HarperCollins, 1991. In Canada at the start of World War Two, Anna faces prejudice that stems from her German heritage while contending with such everyday problems as her first school dance. Challenging.

Lowry, Lois. *Autumn Street.* Houghton Mifflin, 1980; Dell, 1986. Elizabeth is forced to grow up when her father goes to fight in World War Two, her family moves in with her grandfather, and a special friend is struck by tragedy. Challenging.

Lowry, Lois. *Number the Stars.* Houghton Mifflin, 1989; Dell, 1992. The terrors and triumphs of two girls during World War Two in Nazi-occupied Denmark. Newbery Medal. Challenging.

Marko, Katherine M. *Hang Out the Flag.* Macmillian, 1992. A sixth-grade girl tries to come up with a special welcome for her father returning from service overseas. Average.

McSwigan, Marie. *Snow Treasure.* Dutton, 1942; Scholastic, 1986. In 1940, Norwegian children outwit Nazis by sneaking a multimillion dollar cargo of gold bullion onto a freighter. Based on a true story. Challenging.

Mochizuki, Ken. *Baseball Saved Us.* Lee & Low, 1993. "Shorty," interned at a camp for Japanese Americans, finds dignity and acceptance through baseball. Easy.

Fiction *continued*

Orlev, Uri. *The Man from the Other Side.* Houghton Mifflin, 1991. Fourteen-year-old Marek and his family hide Jewish refugees from the Warsaw Ghetto during World War Two. Challenging.

Ray, Deborah K. *My Daddy Was a Soldier: A World War Two Story.* Holiday House, 1990. Life on the American home front is described through the eyes of a girl whose father is a soldier. Average.

Savin, Marcia. *The Moon Bridge.* Scholastic, 1992. Fifth-grader Ruthie struggles to maintain her friendship with her Japanese-American friend Mitzi, even after Mitzi and her family are deported to an internment camp. Average.

Schnur, Steven. *The Shadow Children.* Morrow, 1994. While visiting his grandfather's farm in France, a boy discovers that the ghosts of Jewish children, murdered in World War Two, haunt the woods. Average.

Stevenson, James. *Don't You Know There's a War On?* Greenwillow, 1992. In this illustrated tale, a ten-year-old boy does his part on the home front while his father and brother serve in the military. Easy.

Uchida, Yoshiko. *The Bracelet.* Philomel, 1993. Memories of her best friend help sustain Emi when she and her Japanese-American family are sent to an internment camp. Challenging.

Uchida, Yoshiko. *Journey to Topaz.* Scribners, 1971; Creative Arts Books, 1985. A Japanese-American family is forced to move to two relocation centers. Their discomfort and unfair treatment are seen through the eyes of the young daughter. A sequel to this book is *Journey Home.* Challenging.

Ziefert, Harriet. *A New Coat for Anna.* Knopf, 1986. Anna and her mother must trade possessions to acquire the materials to make a new coat. A story about sacrifice, patience, and values. Average.

Nonfiction

Bachrach, Susan D. *Tell Them We Remember: The Story of the Holocaust.* Little, Brown, 1994. A forceful account of the Holocaust, covering everything from Nazi propaganda to death camps to liberation. Average.

Cohen, Stan. *V for Victory: America's Home Front During World War II.* Pictorial Histories, 1991. A fascinating visual tour of the war years, surveying everything from recruiting to movies to rationing. Challenging.

Dolen, Edward F. *America in World War II: 1941.* Millbrook Press, 1991; Houghton Mifflin, 1994. An account of the bombing of Pearl Harbor and its aftermath. Average.

Hurwitz, Johanna. *Anne Frank: Life in Hiding.* Jewish Publication Society, 1988; Morrow, 1993. A biography of the Jewish girl made famous by the diary she kept during the two years her family hid from the Nazis during World War Two. Challenging.

Litoff, Judy B., and David C. Smith. *Since You Went Away: World War II Letters.* Oxford Univ., 1991. A fascinating collection of letters from American women on the home front to men on the frontlines. Good read-aloud. Challenging.

Morimoto, Junko. *My Hiroshima.* Viking, 1987; Puffin, 1992. A survivor of the first atomic bomb explosion recounts her story of the devastating attack. Easy.

Rosenberg, Maxine B. *Hiding to Survive: Fourteen Jewish Children and the Gentiles Who Rescued Them from the Holocaust.* Clarion, 1994. Survivors of the Holocaust recount the horror and heroism they experienced. Average.

Snyder, Louis L. *World War II.* Franklin Watts, 1981. Important events and people from the war era are introduced through photographs and maps. Challenging.

Stein, R. Conrad. *The Home Front.* Childrens Press, 1986. An overview of life in the United States during World War Two, with photographs and illustrations. Average.

Sullivan, George. *The Day Pearl Harbor Was Bombed: A Photo History of World War II.* Scholastic, 1991. The historic events that occurred before, during, and after the war are presented in a contemporary magazine format. Challenging.

Whitman, Sylvia. *V Is for Victory: The American Homefront During World War II.* Lerner, 1992. This excellent overview of life on the home front discusses civil defense, rationing, propaganda, censorship, Japanese relocation, and racial division. Challenging.

MOLLY'S MAP

Pull out your picture map of Molly's world on the opposite page—carefully, so it doesn't rip!

You can press out the folds by ironing the map. Put tissue paper on one side of the map and press it, using a delicate setting. Press the other side of the map the same way. Keep the iron moving to prevent the map from puckering.